Fire over Ice

A COLLECTION OF POEMS
ABOUT OVERCOMING
EMOTIONAL ABUSE

Sharon Louise Chapman

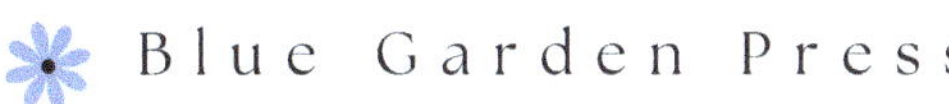
Blue Garden Press

www.bluegardenpress.com

ISBN: 979-8-9953058-0-4

Printed in the United States of America

For Georgie
(2008-2017)

Contents

Contents

Contents

Support Affirmation

"You are held"

PHOTO ©SHARON LOUISE CHAPMAN

Preface

It has taken me many years—and a long, emotional journey—to write this collection of poems and to get to the point where I was ready to publish them. I had no control in writing them. They were an outpouring of my bottled-up grief and emotions from too many years spent within an emotionally abusive relationship.

Once they started pouring out of me, the flood continued for several months. A few of them didn't materialize until about a year or so later. Not all of my poems made it into this book. I chose the best ones that I felt told my journey.

The poems reflect on the beginning of the relationship, travel deep into the darkness of the relationship, and finally retell the breaking free on the other side of it. However, the journey itself was not a linear one.

One of the poems, *Insanity*, was originally published in *The Phoenix Spirit*, a recovery newspaper based in Minneapolis, Minnesota. I would like to thank the publishers of *The Phoenix Spirit*, Aaron and Jen, for their support of my work and my journey over the past several years.

Acknowledging, healing, and recovering from an emotionally abusive relationship is a raw experience. Many years ago, it would not have been talked about as it is today. Yet, we still have a long way to go in recognizing and publicly calling out this type of behavior.

My hope is that publishing this book will help survivors of emotional abuse to feel seen and heard and encourage discussion around the subject. It is not intended to call out a single individual or to lay blame or guilt. This is *my* journey—and my retelling of it and how it made me feel—and one which has taken courage to share.

I encourage you to educate yourself on all types of abuse, learn how you can support and help those going through it, and give either time or resources to both local and national domestic violence organizations. Without them, many—myself included—would not have the resources to figure a way out of what can seem like an impossible situation.

With hope for the future,

Trigger Warning

The poems in this book reference accounts of domestic violence and thoughts of suicide.

National Domestic Violence Hotline: 1-800-799-7233
Suicide and Crisis Hotline: 988

Support Affirmation

"You are worthy"

WORDS

I have no words
to describe the pain
of finding out
it was just a game.

A lofty conquest,
a back street deal,
a badge of honor
that made me feel -
sick to my stomach
and such a fool;
here I was thinking
I'd found a jewel.

But you used your words
to seal the deal
and had me thinking
your love was real.

Words twisted,
and used so wrong;
otherwise you knew
I'd be gone.

But now I write
for a living,
and I no longer have
those misgivings.

So here are my words
to describe that time;
now I know
my life is mine.

DID YOU KNOW?

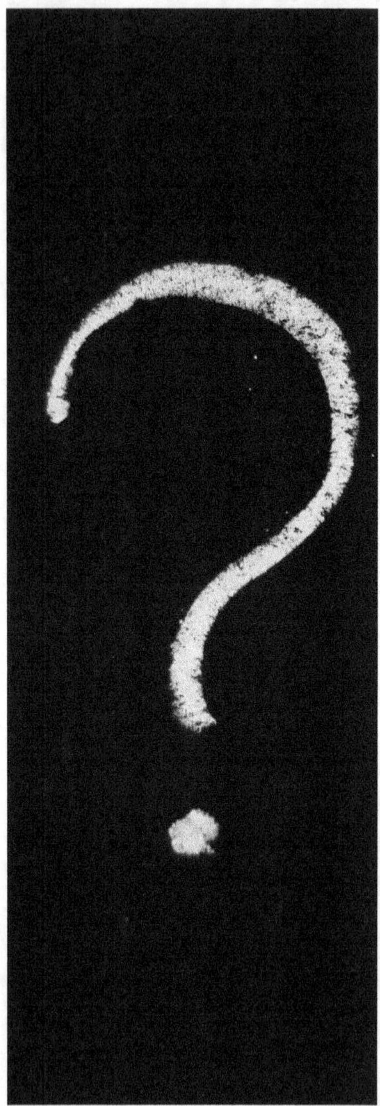

Did you know
how it would go,
the day we kissed
a life we missed?

Did you know?
Was it just a show
to pull me in,
away from kin?

Did you know?
Don't take it slow;
she might reveal
what isn't real.

Did you know
I'd become your foe,
like those before
the life foreseen?

Did you know
I'd write these words?
That I would heal
and be heard?

BEFORE

Before I met you,
before I saw you,
before I dreamed you,
before I knew you

I was happy and free,
loved and adored;
but that was before
I turned up at your door.

Sparkling eyes,
so full of life;
but that was before
I became your wife.

Lovely and lithe,
a laugh and play;
but that was before
my soul was stolen away.

Adventurous and traveled,
confident and true;
but that was before
the day I met you.

PASS ME BY

I pass you on the street,
but we never meet.
You're laughing, young, and hip,
not yet privy to his tricks.

I see the way you look,
clawed in by his hooks;
your life not yet taken,
your mind not yet awakened.

I wish I could tell you how
it would not be all like now.
But would you even listen?
You would say I'm a-dissin'.

Oh, my beautiful one,
don't listen to his song,
siren-like and sweet,
but you'll end up beat.

Yet, I know you'll make it through
and pass me on the street;
for I am you
and you are me-
and that's why we'll never meet.

RUNAWAY BRIDE

Tuesday's child
made a belle bride
on a rainy afternoon
in a late fall monsoon.

Flipflops and blue jeans,
last week's has-beens,
disheveled hair
without a care.

Paperclip and ring,
no outrageous bling.
Swift exchanges of "I do,"
and a quick "I love you."

Runaway bride,
I do thee chide
for the devil you wed,
and took to your bed.

Support Affirmation

“You are free”

PHOTO ©SHARON LOUISE CHAPMAN

SOULLESS

Beautiful girl
when will you see
that he is not
all he claims to be?

The false smile,
the cozy nights in,
all a hook
on the road to sin.

Just like a flash,
he will start to bash
your soul, your life,
cut like a knife.

The demands, the tantrums,
the drink-fueled rants,
only worsen
if you tell him he can't.

The monster inside,
hidden from prying eyes,
will be reserved for you
and everything that you do.

Wake up, wake up,
my pretty one,
before you realize
your life is gone.

BEHIND THE SMILE

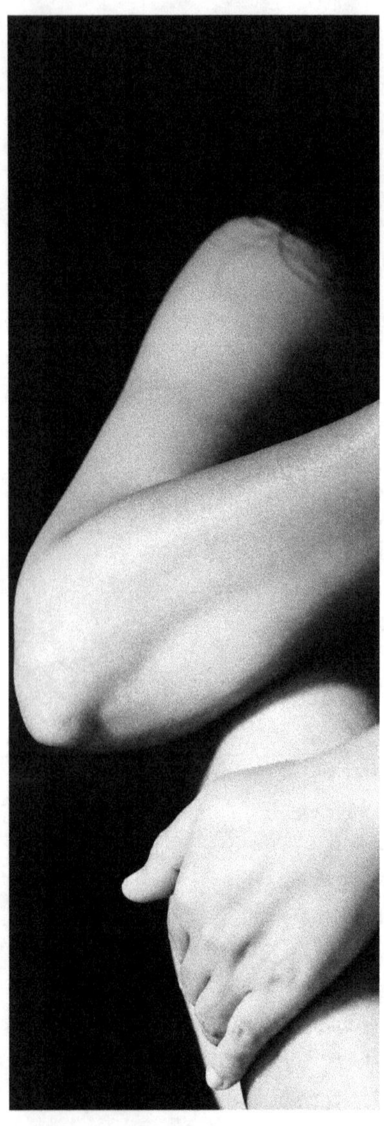

Morning breaks,
my body wakes,
red hot skin.
What lies within?

Pounding head;
enough said!
Good or bad,
it makes me sad.

Does it hurt,
down in the dirt,
where you left me,
after you bled me?

Hidden abuse.
What's the use?
No one believes
he did the deed.

But I bear the scars,
deep within;
my body reminds me
with constant din.

Repeat. Pause. Play.
How goes my day?
Turn up that dial
behind the smile.

And so it goes.

CHAOS

Up, down,
square, round,
left, right,
black, white.

Happy, sad,
happy, mad,
throw dirt,
make it hurt.

Do time,
no dimes,
in charge,
livin' large.

Bam, scam!
"Thank you, ma'am!"
He's the boss.
That's chaos.

DEVIL INSIDE

Black, white,
let's have a fight,
just because
you can't give a toss.

Make her cry,
watch her die,
down in the dirt
for an innocent flirt.

Then online
to watch some porn,
regain control,
leaving her torn.

Eggshells broken,
now she's woken,
never again,
betrayal end.

THE CYCLE

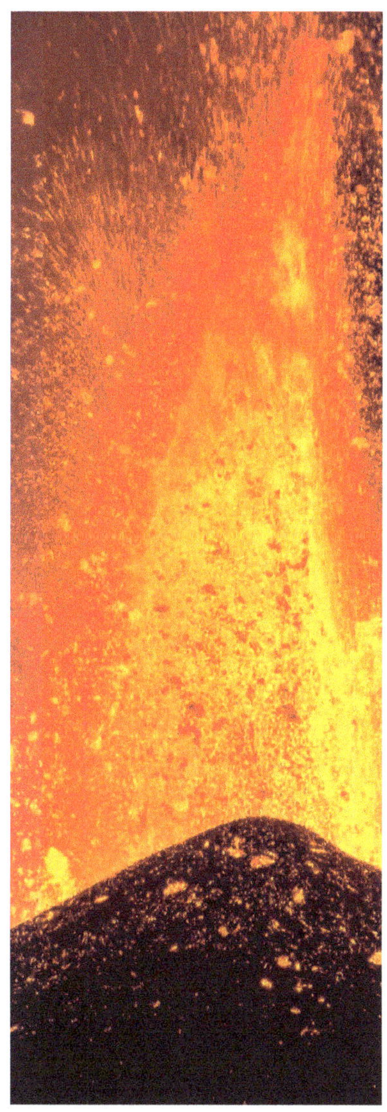

Tick, tock,
goes the clock,
counting down,
never stop.

Furious pacing,
all the waiting,
volcano high,
no reason why.

Odd socks,
cork pops,
compliment miss,
angry hiss.

Time bomb,
all the aplomp,
quick retreat,
I am beat.

Fascination,
no vacation,
I'm out,
no more spout.

Support Affirmation

"You are loved"

PHOTO ©SHARON LOUISE CHAPMAN

BROKEN TOY

Shiny and new,
pleasuring you,
exciting to touch,
treasure and push.

All the right moves,
acting them out,
this one's for keeps,
without a doubt.

One day she breaks,
no noise she makes,
older and sadder,
"How long have you had her?"

Time to replace,
pick up the pace,
new and improved,
not in a mood.

Showing her off
to all who will listen,
not realizing that
she'll soon be imprisoned.

The cycle moves on,
again and again,
it's not a matter of if,
but more like when.

SIGHT UNSEEN

Through the dark,
ne'er a spark
of grimy gray,
yet to pay.

Gold and black,
up they stack,
ne'er seen,
but still they mean.

Blue and mauve,
room to pause,
beautiful you,
I undo.

Just because,
it never was
on display,
I still do pay.

Patterned bruises
in my head,
still so real.
What's the deal?

Shimmering welts
that never melt,
stay with me,
never let it be.

LOCK AND KEY

Love lost,
love found;
don't give me
the runaround.

I am yours,
you are mine,
the only one
with whom I'll dine.

Lock and key,
all about me;
don't you dare
to even share.

Run away?
No, you'll stay!
Until I'm through,
you'll do as I say.

Why so sad?
Don't be mad
that I've taken
everything you had.

What no more?
There's the door!
I'm moving on
to another one.

It's been fun
but now I'm done,
no backward look
at the life I took.

Support Affirmation

"You are seen"

PHOTO ©SHARON LOUISE CHAPMAN

LAY ME DOWN

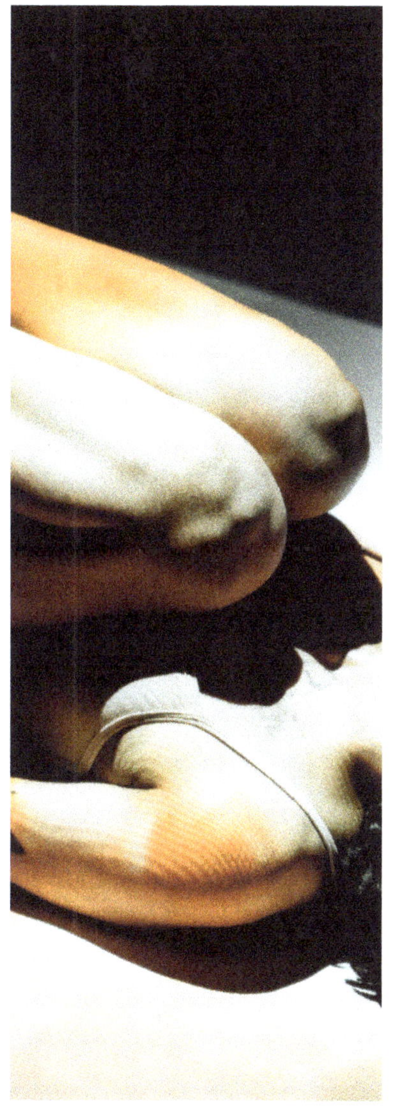

Some days I want to give up the fight,
on days I've fought with all my might.
The pain, the exhaustion, the tired eyes -
my body just continues to sigh.

To lay me down and go to sleep,
so that I no longer have to weep,
perfect sleep and perfect peace,
and all the pain would then cease.

To run through fields of beautiful herbs;
for that I do not have the words.
A dream come true, that would be,
but in this existence I would no longer be.

On days like this when I have no strength,
I sit and cry, and cry again;
inside out and outside in,
is it easier to let you win?

VALENTINE BRIDE

Bleed you dry,
don't ask why,
suck your soul,
left unwhole.

Nightmare dreams,
woken by screams,
such a jerk,
won't make it work.

Shotgun bride,
on the side,
tears of pain,
it starts again.

Snakely eyes,
fearful smiles,
I want out,
I have no doubt.

True self seen,
where you been?
Close the door,
broke to the core.

ME TOO

Boundaries crossed,
lines broken,
privileges taken,
words not spoken.

Touching, probing,
hands a-poking,
down my top -
when will it stop?

Permission denied,
I cannot hide.
"I have a right!"
is your excuse,
as your hands
wander loose.

Misty tears,
all my fears,
lying in bed -
who did I wed?

I have a voice.
"It is my choice!"
Together strong
against this wrong.

The battle cry
goes up so high,
marching on,
however long.

Stop this madness,
halt the sadness;
it's what you do -
me too.

INSANITY

Sex, drink, drugs,
girls, boys, thugs,
on and on it goes,
forever in the flow.

Oh, can't you see
what you did to me?
My face wears the lines
of all your crimes.

Boxed deep inside,
eyes open wide,
why can't I shout
and let it all out?

Botched jobs,
hodge, podge,
so much craziness,
so much haziness.

Such is the life
of an abused wife.
But no more -
I am broken to the core.

Finally I flee
and leave you be
to your world of insanity
and of profanity.

Now at peace,
oh, the release!
A life reclaimed
and no more pain.

Originally published in *The Phoenix Spirit*, July/Aug 2022, Minneapolis, MN

Support Affirmation

"You are safe"

PHOTO ©SHARON LOUISE CHAPMAN

ONCE OR TWICE

Once or twice,
I took my life,
stood on the ledge,
tip toe on edge.

Once or twice,
I rolled the dice;
could I dare?
How would I fare?

But it pulled me back,
up did stack;
you're a tiny piece
for a deadly release.

I soldiered on,
'til I grew strong,
and far away
from such a fateful day.

I tell this tale,
so others won't fail;
hold my hand,
together we band.

Against such games
that drive you insane,
and twisted truth
from the uncouth.

No more ledge,
no more edge.
More than twice?
No! My life is worth thrice!

LIQUOR GOLD

Whiskey fumes,
I am doomed,
always win,
wager sin.

Liquor gold,
he is sold,
love lost,
at all cost.

Crazy eyes,
pie in sky,
dollars flushed,
with a cuss.

I spoke the words,
and you heard,
broke my heart,
so we did part.

ONE NIGHT

Who are you?
Who leaves me blue?
Hands over my head
and playing dead.

Who are you,
pounding on me,
as I sleep,
as I weep?

Who are you,
who claims to know
but offers no words
or tears that flow?

Who are you,
blank as a slate?
Are you really the same
man I did date?

Who are you,
who offers no care,
as I die inside
and lay here bare?

Who are you?
I really don't know,
so in the end,
I had to go.

AFTER THE STORM

Softly falling,
your name a'calling,
tears of grief,
tears of relief.

Pitter, patter,
what's the matter?
Not again?
My dear sweet friend...

Leave him now,
leave him how?
Deeply entwined,
it's not mine.

A crash of thunder,
then a blunder,
huge black downpour,
I can take no more.

See the sun set,
the days our eyes met,
through the storm,
away from norm.

Clearing through,
what can you do?
Walking out there,
without a care.

Shadowed rain,
clears the pain,
fresh new start,
as we do part.

BURNED

Burned on,
In and out,
I am yours,
there is no doubt.

Seared through,
black and blue,
there is nothing
that you can do.

A mark of the devil
scorches the soul
and removes a part
of the whole.

Yet time heals,
on go the wheels,
water and oil
soothe the coils.

Scorched fades,
a whole remade,
but I won't forget
this biggest debt.

LOST AND FOUND

I lost myself
immersed in you;
there wasn't anything
that I wouldn't do.

To jump through hoops,
again and again,
it didn't matter
where or when.

Your soul and mine
became just one;
oh, how could I
be so wrong?

I invested myself
in soul, body and mind,
and in the end,
you couldn't be kind.

I bought you everything
your heart desired,
even when of me,
you grew tired.

I was lost,
completely at sea,
and didn't know
who else to be.

In deep grief
of losing myself,
I had no life,
and nothing I felt.

The voice,
it wouldn't go away,
at first a whisper,
and then every day.

You can be,
so much more than this!
A life of passion,
and not a fake kiss.

Find yourself
before it's too late,
and you are
consumed by your fate.

And so no more
duty bound;
yes, I was lost,
but now I'm found.

UP FROM THE DIRT

Down in the dirt,
Oh, God, it hurts!
Disheveled and torn,
looked at with scorn.

You put me here,
the price was dear;
I paid the toll,
fell down the hole.

Narcissistic pride,
eyes open wide,
how do you exist
and live like this?

Bring down what's true,
domineered by false you;
the filthy truth,
how do I undo?

But I see you now,
ran as fast as I could,
took me ten long years
to become who I should.

I am now empowered
about your kind;
run, run, run,
before he takes your mind.

Support Affirmation

"You are strong"

PATTERNS

Love bomb,
heart's won,
perfect guy,
I am high.

Next stage,
turn the page,
now the abuse -
what's the use?

First the explosion,
now the silence,
on for days,
make her pay.

Start over,
life of clover,
toe the line,
until it's time.

On again,
new friend,
new love,
rise above.

Finally out,
don't pout!
Lucky you-
life anew.

NUMBER 4

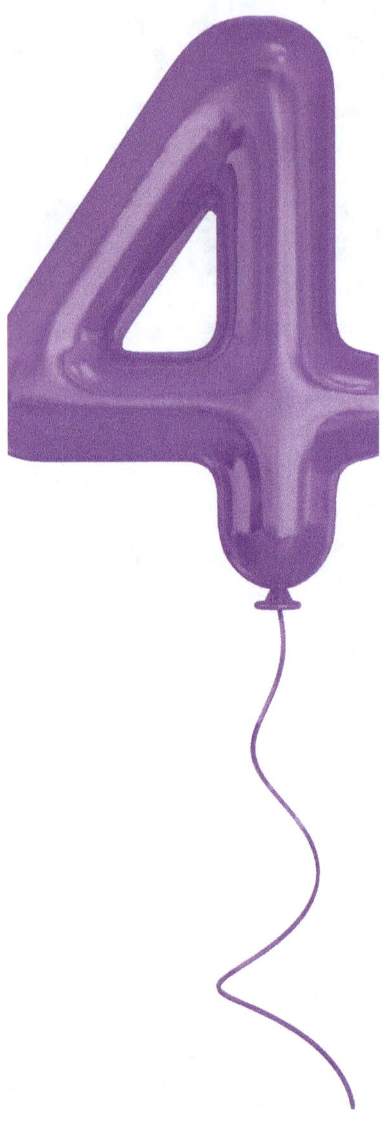

Number four
said no more,
all the stress,
what a mess.

You want money,
I want honey.
You want deals,
I want real.

Cat fishing,
dirt a'dishing,
another caught,
another bought.

Treat her good,
as you should;
treat her bad,
oh, so sad.

Little boys
with their toys -
I want this,
I want that.

But number four
saw the door,
grabbed her pack,
didn't look back.

THE CROSSING

Burning bridges,
black witches,
never found,
what confounds.

Hard to believe,
watch you seethe,
melt and pour,
not no more.

I watch and listen,
scared to christen,
pure white lie,
I'd rather die.

Dead inside,
what a ride,
cross the river,
body quiver.

Safe at last,
a dark, sad past,
but now in front
and not the runt.

Full wolf moon,
gone so soon,
no more meddle,
goodbye devil.

WINTER NIGHT

Cold as winter,
across the veil,
all the effort,
it does entail.

An outstretched hand,
pale and white,
grabs me strongly,
with all its might.

Across the veil,
through the mist,
I catch a glimpse,
a ghostly wisp.

Is it true,
what you do?
In a rage,
so fast you flew.

Green and white,
fog be bound,
I whisper softly,
but no sound.

A laugh, a smirk,
a stolen look,
followed by
a flying book.

I break free,
one cold night,
through ghostly moon
and the light.

No backward glance,
no regret -
I'll never miss you;
don't you fret.

FIRE OVER ICE

Ice over fire,
down in the mire,
drown out the flames
of all her gains.

Melt her passion,
melt her ambition -
after all,
you wouldn't want her wishing

Of a life of her own
that you couldn't condone,
she wouldn't be then there
to carry out your cares.

But fire over ice
can make you think twice;
rise up from wet flames
and over all of the pain.

Flames in the sky,
rising so high,
sizzle out the ice
with all of her spice.

Support Affirmation

"You are fire"

PHOTO ©SHARON LOUISE CHAPMAN

PUSH

Push her down,
up she rises,
no more lies
or disguises.

Now she sees you,
dark and true;
what are you
going to do?

All the rage,
all the anger,
out and out,
her you chew.

Escape, escape
from the hate!
There you are,
standing raging.

Shout her out,
mock her, hurt her;
she's black and blue,
but now she sees you!

She is free,
wild once more -
no longer that abused girl
on your floor.

FROZEN

Frozen in time,
like a leaf in ice,
you hurt me once,
then twice and thrice.

I couldn't move,
convinced that you'd see,
all of the damage
you inflicted on me.

But just like ice
on a frozen pond,
your gaze so thick,
I knew I'd been conned.

The past wasn't what
I thought it to be;
turn the lock,
and throw away the key.

I cried and screamed
and pounded in despair;
the look you had
was not one of care.

The ice melted,
and I finally felt it -
black and dark,
empty and stark.

I gingerly moved,
despite being bruised;
pains and sores,
I could take it no more.

The sun rose
over the cold, grey dawn,
and now I know
I am no longer your pawn

From ice to water,
flowing and knowing,
onward it pours;
I'm frozen no more.

RISE

I will rise from the depths of the deepest sea,
up and up from where you left me be;
I will arc like the breach of the mighty whale,
and soar in the sky,
breaking free from my jail.

You tried to break me,
remold me,
shape me;
but my soul survived,
and the tortured me died.

I will rise to be strong,
beautiful, empowered,
no more in the corner,
broken and cowered.

Up, up, up from the deep, black sea,
returned to the place
where I am me.

FIRE

Fire hot,
fire cold,
streaks of blue,
red and gold.

Burn bright,
burn strong,
burn gently,
burn long.

You are fire,
not in mire,
mighty strong,
all day long.

Cast a spell,
all is well,
light a spark,
no more dark.

THIEF

Money and gold,
man of old,
beautiful girls,
all in a whirl.

Silver tongue,
hearts won,
all a game,
to you, the same.

Tattered and torn,
all forlorn -
do you care?
Is it fair?

Lives you stole,
all a goal,
moving on!
This one is done.

End of the line,
now it's mine,
no more fog,
me and my dog.

SCORCHED SOUL

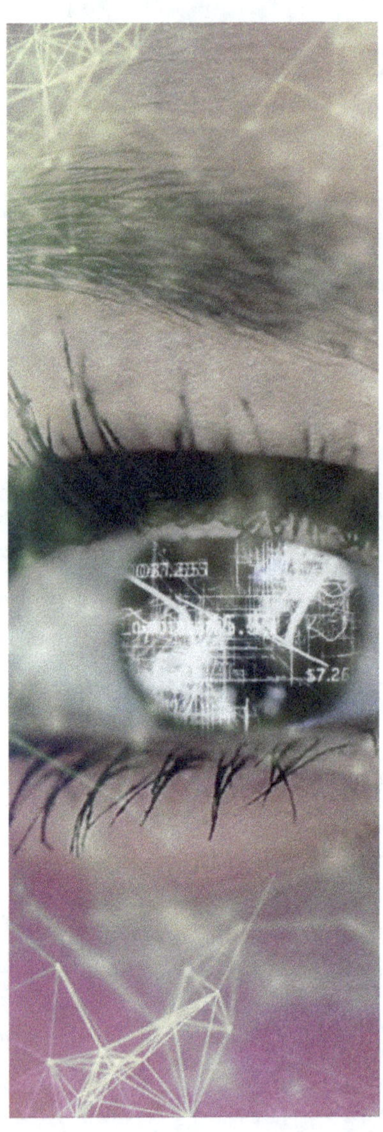

Deep inside
where the pain lies,
you removed my soul
and scorched a hole.

You got in my head
and left me for dead;
I sit and wait,
resigned to my fate.

But now no more,
I slam shut that door,
nail it up tight,
with all my might.

I rediscover my soul,
make it whole,
with love and time;
now it's all mine.

Support Affirmation

"You are whole"

ICE

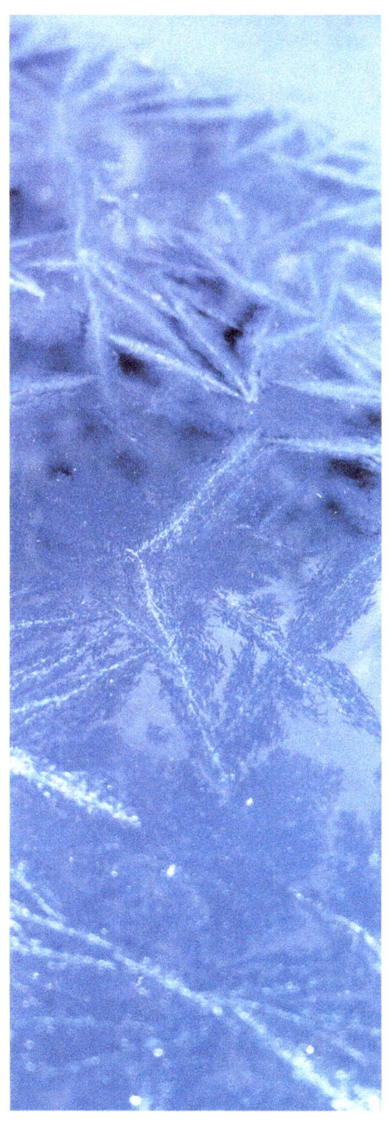

Icy blue flowing through my veins
of a love that once was feigned,
red hot blue, through and through,
and I was lost in the mirage of you.

Cold and white, black as night,
all at once, the sun shone bright,
crisp and cold, shades of blue
melted with the nuanced you.

Water glimmers, ice shimmers -
how could I have not seen?
Cold and dead, in my bed,
freezing out what could have been.

The ice melts
the painful welts;
warming sun healing through
the icy glass, it comes to pass -
no more pain, no more you.

BROKEN WING

Like a caged bird
that cannot sing,
you left me
with a broken wing.

Deep inside
my body rages,
like the words
on these pages.

Attack! Attack!
My body screams,
all the time
or so it seems.

Constant pain,
oh, so tired!
You left me quickly
and deeply mired.

A broken wing
does not serve
the narcissistic desires
of a twisted perv.

But a bird with a wing,
broken or not,
never stays tethered
to the same spot.

You left me bruised,
battered and torn,
but the old me
I will not mourn.

She taught me how
not to survive,
but how to adapt
and how to thrive.

So broken wing,
lift me high,
through the mire
and to the sky.

And look upon
that old abuse;
it served its purpose
and now has no use.

Now I thrive,
although sick inside,
and in these words
I do confide:

You are beautiful,
you are strong,
despite the one
who did you wrong.

UNBOUND

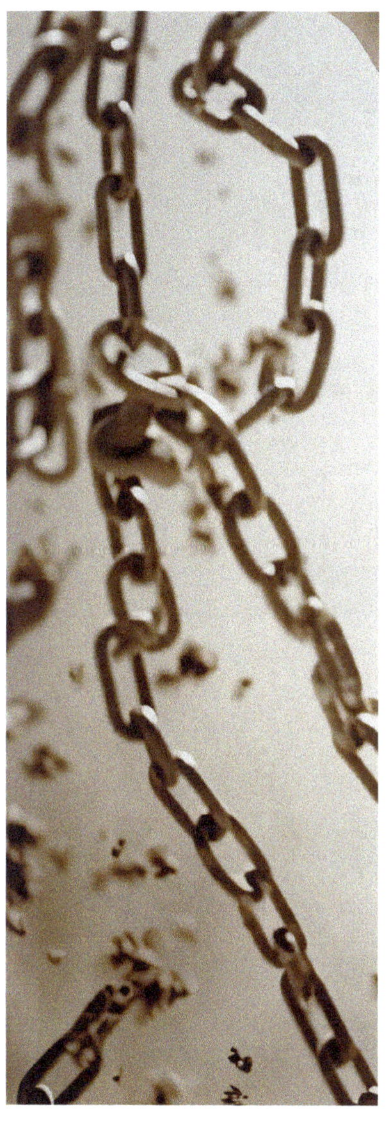

Chains of rust,
chains of gold,
doesn't matter,
truth be told.

Chains are chains,
dust is dust;
bind me up,
if you must.

But one day soon,
without a sound,
from these chains,
I'll come unbound.

Away from you,
fast and free,
uplifting wings,
help me flee.

Broken chains,
broken bounds -
it doesn't matter,
if you pound.

No longer afraid,
no more fear,
I'll rise above you,
far and clear.

PIECES OF ME

Pieces of me
scattered over the ground,
digging down deep,
digging around.

A lost piece here,
a lost piece there -
where did it go?
How did I not miss it so?

Smashed apart
by a broken heart -
can I ever fix
all these broken bits?

But one by one,
ten by ten,
all of a sudden,
they're on the mend.

You can break me
and shape me,
a hand maiden on show,
but bury my soul?
What? Hell, no!

DIRT

On the ground
down and out,
your steely gaze,
your angry pout.

Black as dirt,
so much hurt,
I dare not move,
I dare not soothe.

Crushed and powdered,
brown and soft,
red-black gold
of stories told.

Mushed and gritty,
food for flowers -
dirt has history,
dirt has power.

Build a fortress?
Build a tower?
No, with this dirt,
I'll build my power.

LOSING ME

Beneath the stars,
beneath the trees
where I left
a piece of me.

Long since buried,
favor curried,
I left it there,
without a care.

I wandered lost,
to what cost;
I couldn't find
what I hid.

Then through the boughs
of laden leaves,
all at once,
I did see

that piece I lost,
threw out and tossed,
had grown sky high,
and did not die.

For through the war
of pain and more,
it had grown stronger,
mighty and longer.

Now it fitted
back with me,
no longer lost,
but wild and free.

TWILIGHT FIRE

Twist, turn,
watch her burn,
tied tight,
despite her fight.

Yes, sire,
what you desire,
no thoughts,
she's bought.

No escape,
that's her fate,
fire out,
all in drought.

One seed
is all it takes;
now she's fighting
against those stakes.

Mighty passion,
no longer rationed,
burns the ropes,
and ignites hope.

On fire,
raging red,
all exploding
in her head.

I am me,
don't you see?
Never smother
the passion of another.

Words do flow
and now you know,
she did rise
and now so wise.

Twilight stars
shine so bright,
fire burning
in the night.

Support Affirmation

"You are passion"

RAW

I am raw,
cut to the core,
wounded in flight,
hidden from sight.

I am raw;
I am me no more,
lost in the haze
of those crazy days.

I am raw,
crippled with gore,
an unwelcome look;
here I am stuck.

I am raw,
afraid of the door,
no confidence to date,
consumed by your hate.

Will it ever stop?
Will the bubble burst
so one day I might
soar back to great heights?

To be held and to be loved,
without being shoved,
a kiss and a hug,
all warm and snug.

Maybe it will,
maybe it won't,
but at least I am free,
free to be me.

AFTER

Whiskey breath
and crazy eyes,
inside of me,
silent cries.

Make it stop
before a pop
of beer and hurt,
and up my skirt.

I long for peace
of a normal life,
a day of laughter
and not a fight.

To learn to sing,
so loud, so proud,
and to eat ice-cream
without being cowed.

The fragrance of
a soft, pink rose,
some digging time
and blissful doze.

Just humdrum things
I now do treasure
without mind-bending tactics
and crazy weather.

Not a sound,
nor a pound
of slamming doors,
or listening for
angry caws.

Fear gone,
heart's song,
now so tranquil;
yes, this is after.

NEW VOYAGE

You broke me hard,
you broke me good,
you broke me like
a piece of wood.

Splintered and torn,
ragged and worn;
how to fix
this huge, huge mix?

But piece by piece
with screw and nail,
I eventually was
ready to sail.

The cracks they healed
with ridges grooved -
it is something
you should behoove.

Despite the breaks
splintered and worn,
I went on to shine,
onto another new dawn.

Better than new,
better than you,
no more maiden,
beaten my Satan.

To horizons new,
far and wide,
having a reason
to hold my head up with pride.

Support Affirmation

"You are heard"

BLUE

Sometimes I'm blue
because of you,
the things you did,
the things you hid.

Sometimes I'm blue,
don't know what to do,
not good enough to be here,
or to have someone near.

Sometimes I'm blue,
and I can't see what's true,
what's now right in my life,
free of trouble and strife.

A different shade of blue,
not the blackest of blue,
but of the great sky,
one I can ride so high.

Up in the stars,
up so far,
that's my new blue,
happy and true.

BEAUTIFUL BOY

PHOTO
©SHARON LOUISE
CHAPMAN

Your reign of terror
has come to an end,
but it has been so
hard to mend.

My broken heart,
my long-gone mate,
it's hard to not
be consumed by hate.

My four-legged friend
was all to me;
why couldn't you
just let it be?

Jealous rage
and hate-filled eyes -
constant rants
did make him pant.

My little warrior
true and true,
it wasn't anything
that you did do.

I miss you so
now you are gone -
no beautiful boy
sitting in the sun.

But now you're safe
when I couldn't help you be,
and one day again
each other we'll see.

BURIED

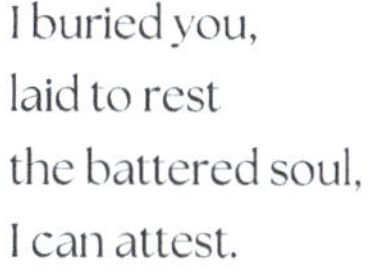

I buried you,
laid to rest
the battered soul,
I can attest.

Tired and worn,
a weary ghost
who fought so hard
against the most.

Sleep, sweet sleep,
my precious one;
your work here
is now all done.

I AM THE VOICE

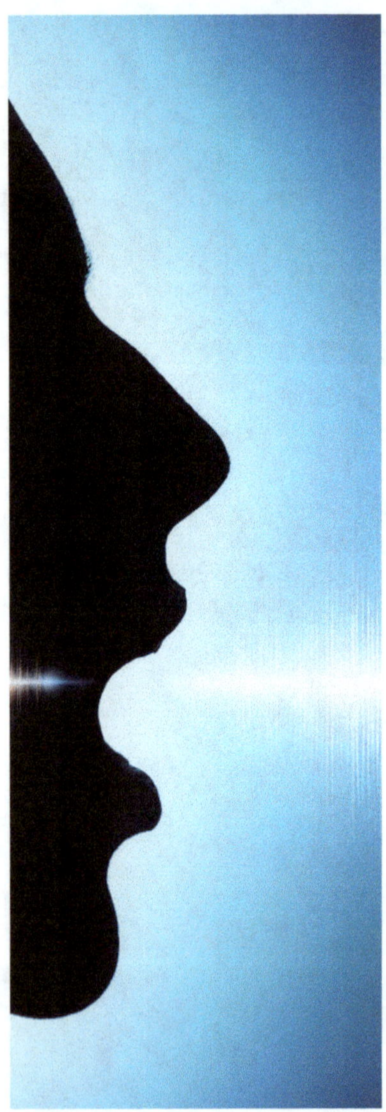

I am the voice
inside your head,
the one that niggles
when you go to bed.

"You know you hurt me,"
it taunts so slow;
"Do you think
that I can let that go?"

It rises up
when you have no choice;
yes, listen closely,
I am the voice.

Support Affirmation

"You are healed"

THE END

At the end,
will they ask,
as you take
your last gasp?

At the end,
who will be there?
And if they are,
will they care?

At the end
when night draws in,
will you still wear
that steely grin?

At the end,
how will you cope?
If no one's there,
will you lose hope?

At the end,
will you reflect
on lives discarded
and those you kept?

At the end,
I will not mock
as the minutes
tick on the clock.

At the end,
I will only pray
that we never meet
another day.

I can forgive
but not forget,
at the end,
the day we met.

www.ingramcontent.com/pod-product-compliance
Lightning Source LLC
LaVergne TN
LVHW010615110826
845149LV00003B/925

* 9 7 9 8 9 9 5 3 0 5 8 0 4 *